CHRISTMAS CREATIONS

Published by Blackbirch Press, Inc.
260 Amity Road
Woodbridge, CT 06525

©2000 by Blackbirch Press, Inc.
First Edition

Originally published as: *Crea Movitos de Navidad* by Anna Llimós and Laia Sadurni.
Photography by Nos y Soto; illustrations by Nuria Giralt.

Original Copyright: ©1997 Parramón Ediciones, S.A., World Rights, Published by Parramón Ediciones, S.A., Barcelona, Spain.

e-mail: staff@blackbirch.com
Web site: www.blackbirch.com

Printed in Spain

10 9 8 7 6 5 4 3 2 1

Library of Congress Cataloging-in-Publication Data
Llimós, Anna.
[Crea motivos de Navidad. English]
Christmas Creations / by Anna Llimós and Laia Sadurni.
    p.   cm. — (Crafts for all seasons)
Includes index.
Summary: Provides instructions for creating various Christmas crafts, decorations, cards, and gift wrappings.
ISBN 1-56711-437-7 (hardcover : alk. paper)
1. Christmas decorations—Juvenile literature. [1. Christmas decorations. 2. Handicraft.] I. Sadurni, Laia. II. Title. III. Crafts for all seasons (Woodbridge, Conn.)
TT900 .C4 L59   2000   00-008583
745.594'12—dc21   CIP
                                              AC

Contents

✂ = Adult supervision strongly recommended

CRAFTS FOR ALL SEASONS

CHRISTMAS CREATIONS

BLACKB, INC.

WOODBRIDGE, CONNECTICUT

Wildlife Wrapping

☞ YOU'LL NEED:
**shiny paper,
crepe paper, construction paper,
colored pencils,
different-colored
adhesive tape, and
scissors.**

1. Wrap the gift in shiny paper.

2. Tie a crepe paper bow around the package.

3. Draw the head, legs, and tail of a giraffe on construction paper.

4. Cut out the giraffe pieces and draw spots on them with a colored pencil. Draw the nose, mouth, and eyes on the head.

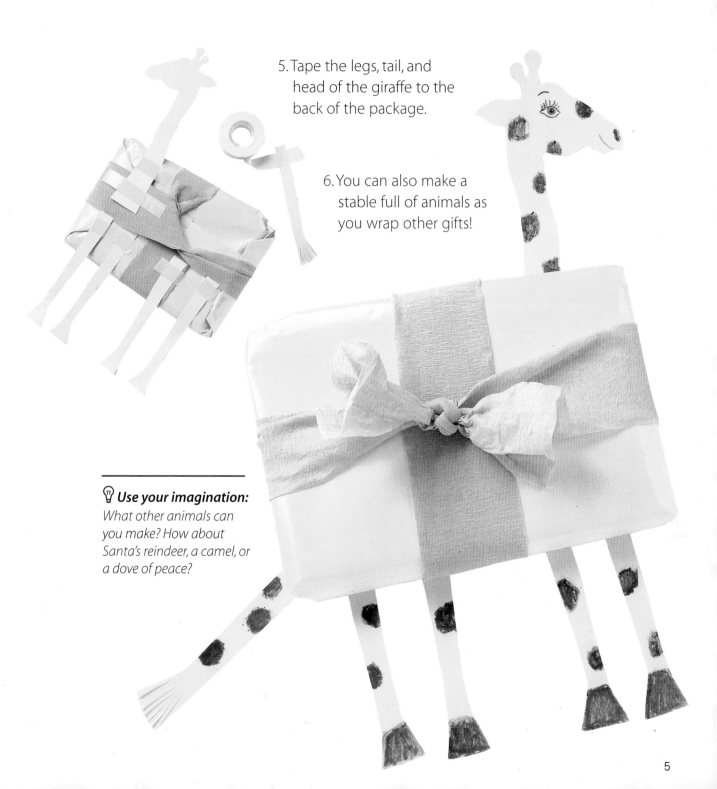

5. Tape the legs, tail, and head of the giraffe to the back of the package.

6. You can also make a stable full of animals as you wrap other gifts!

💡 *Use your imagination:*
What other animals can you make? How about Santa's reindeer, a camel, or a dove of peace?

5

A Camel Bearing Gifts

☛ **YOU'LL NEED: two paper tubes, tissue paper, construction paper, crayons, glue, colored adhesive tape, scissors, and a black marker.**

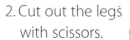

1. Draw legs on the two paper tubes as shown.

2. Cut out the legs with scissors.

3. Glue the two tubes together so that both sets of feet are facing forward.

4. Draw the head of a camel on construction paper.

5. Cut out the head and color it.

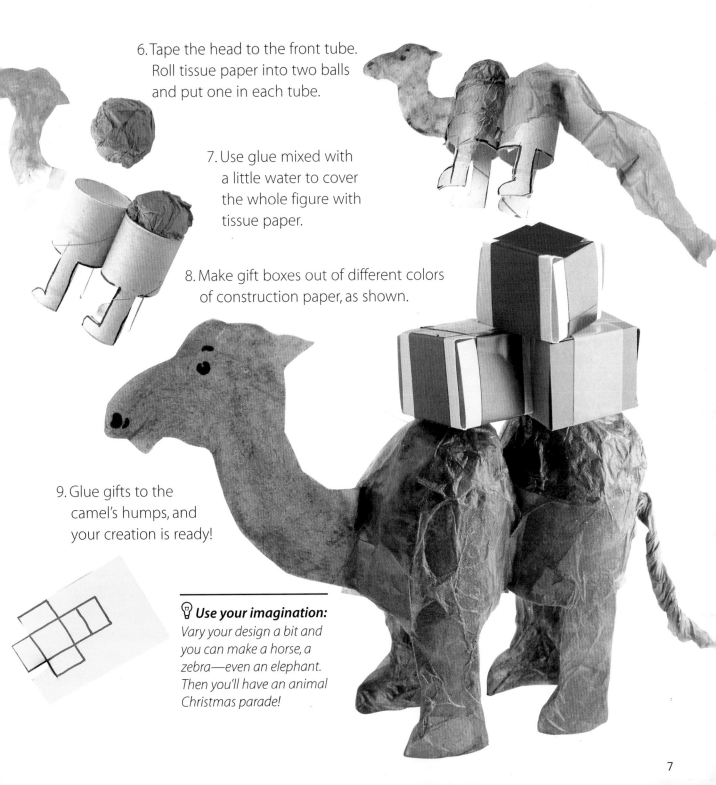

6. Tape the head to the front tube. Roll tissue paper into two balls and put one in each tube.

7. Use glue mixed with a little water to cover the whole figure with tissue paper.

8. Make gift boxes out of different colors of construction paper, as shown.

9. Glue gifts to the camel's humps, and your creation is ready!

💡 *Use your imagination:*
Vary your design a bit and you can make a horse, a zebra—even an elephant. Then you'll have an animal Christmas parade!

Spectacular Sparkly Ornaments

☞ *YOU'LL NEED: newspapers, adhesive tape, paper clips, tissue paper, glue, glitter, and ribbon.*

1. Make a ball out of newspaper.

2. Take a paper clip and open it up. Stick one end into the newspaper ball and tape it in place.

3. Use glue mixed with a little water to cover the ball with tissue paper. You can use one color or combine different colors.

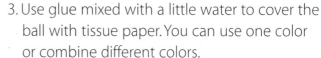

4. Before the glue
dries, sprinkle the
ball with glitter.

5. Tie a ribbon to
the paper clip.

6. Now you're ready to
hang your ornament
on your tree!

💡 *Use your imagination:*
You can vary the shapes
you make by changing or
lengthening the newspa-
per shape. Try gluing some
newspaper spikes onto the
ball for a starlike shape!

Tree with a Twist

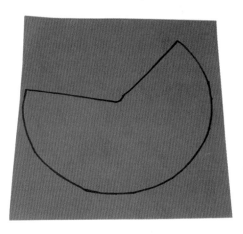

☞ **YOU'LL NEED:**
glossy paper, glue,
construction paper,
paint, scissors, and
an old toothbrush.

1. On green construction paper, draw two-thirds of a circle.

2. Cut out the shape and use glue to make a cone.

3. Cut out various shapes from different-colored glossy papers.

10

4. Use a toothbrush to sprinkle white paint on the cone. It will look as if snow has fallen on the tree.

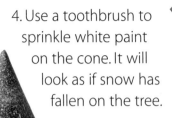

5. Cut a spiral out of a sheet of construction paper.

6. Decorate the spiral with paint.

7. Glue the center of the spiral onto the tip of the tree. Watch your Christmas tree mobile bob and turn in the breeze!

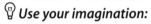

💡 *Use your imagination:*
How about making Santa's road home to the North Pole? Or how about a winding roadway up a steep mountain?

Wonderful Wire Figures

☛ **YOU'LL NEED:** *fine wire or a pipe cleaner, colored adhesive tape, glue, construction paper, paint, a paintbrush, glitter, and scissors.*

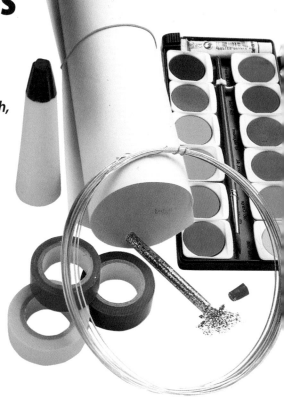

1. Bend the wire to form a loop as shown.

2. Use colored adhesive tape to cover the entire wire, except for the loop at the top.

3. Draw a star or other shape on construction paper.

4. Place another sheet of construction paper under the first and cut out a second star.

5. Paint each star a bright color.

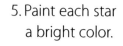

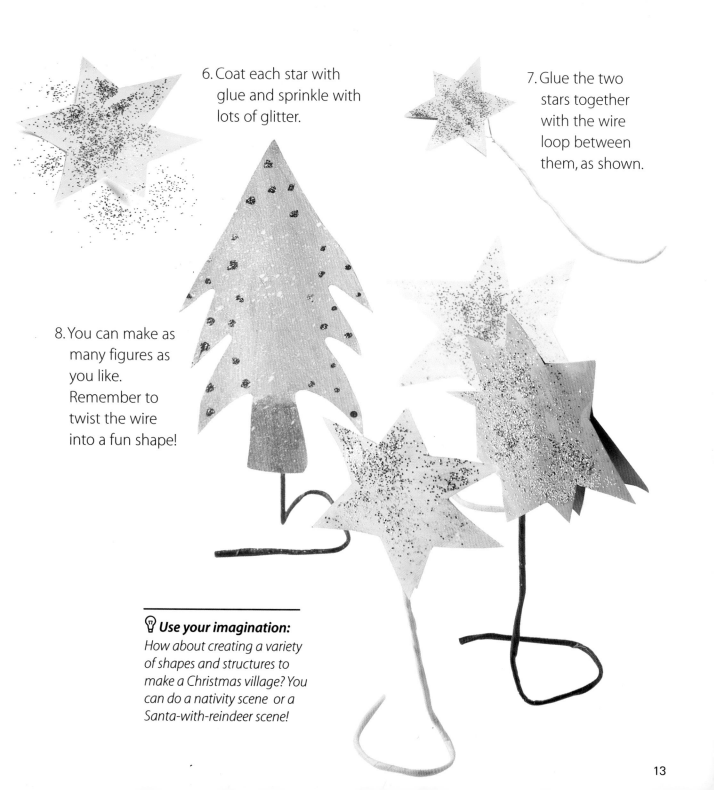

6. Coat each star with glue and sprinkle with lots of glitter.

7. Glue the two stars together with the wire loop between them, as shown.

8. You can make as many figures as you like. Remember to twist the wire into a fun shape!

💡 *Use your imagination:*
How about creating a variety of shapes and structures to make a Christmas village? You can do a nativity scene or a Santa-with-reindeer scene!

Glamorous Gift Bag

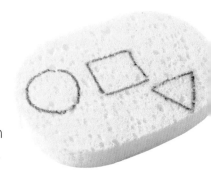

☛ **YOU'LL NEED: a cardboard box, paint, a sponge, construction paper, string, adhesive tape, wrapping paper, glue, and scissors.**

1. Paint the cardboard box.

2. Choose two opposite sides of the box. Out of colored construction paper, cut two rectangles that are longer and wider than the sides of the box.

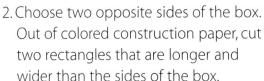

3. Cut zig-zag patterns on two edges of the rectangles. Tape string to the top of each rectangle for handles.

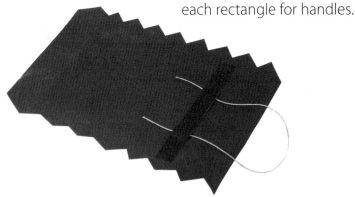

4. Draw different shapes on a sponge.

5. Cut out the shapes and use them as stamps. Dip one end of the stamp in paint and press it on the construction paper to make a design.

6. Glue the decorated rectangles to opposite sides of the box.

7. You can also cover the rectangles with wrapping paper.

💡 *Use your imagination: Experiment with other textures dipped in paint. Try string, twigs, or the tip of an eraser. You can also glue various items to the outside, to add a three-dimensional look.*

Crafty Cards ✂

☛ **YOU'LL NEED:**
construction paper, pastel crayons or chalk, a utility knife, and glue.

1. Draw a Christmas design on a sheet of white construction paper.

2. Have an adult cut out the design with a utility knife.

3. Use pastel crayons to draw lines that follow the outline of the cut-out shape.

4. Place the outlined piece face-up on construction paper. Rub the pastel color into the opening with your finger.

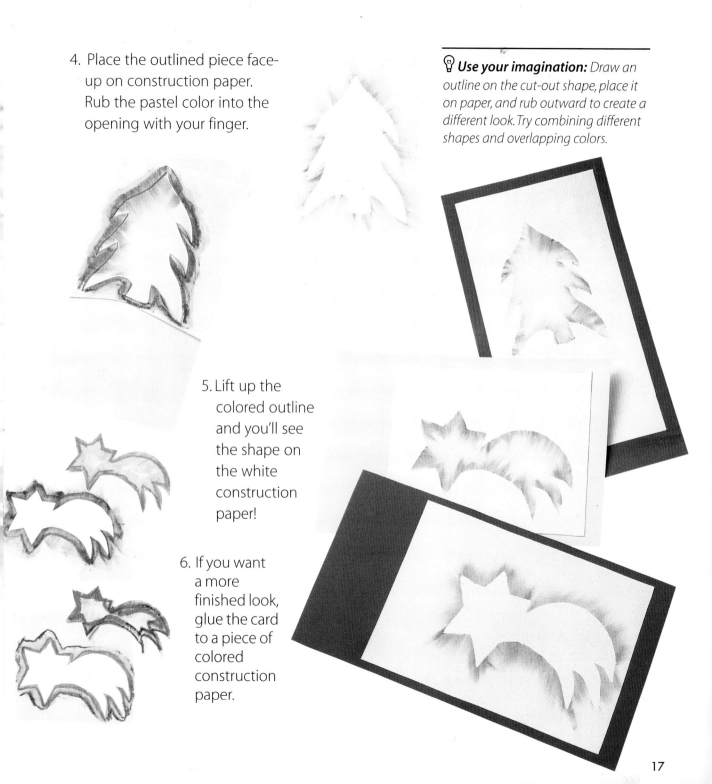

💡 **Use your imagination:** *Draw an outline on the cut-out shape, place it on paper, and rub outward to create a different look. Try combining different shapes and overlapping colors.*

5. Lift up the colored outline and you'll see the shape on the white construction paper!

6. If you want a more finished look, glue the card to a piece of colored construction paper.

Spunky Santa on a String

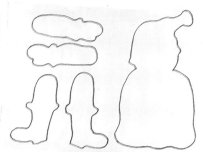

☛ *YOU'LL NEED: construction paper, felt, brads, glue, string, cotton, scissors, paint, and a black marker.*

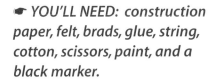

1. On thick construction paper, draw the head, body, arms, and legs of a Santa Claus, as shown.

2. Cut out the pieces. Make four small holes, and place brads in the corners of the body. Also, make two small holes in each arm and leg.

3. Glue on red felt for a hat and clothing. Leave the hands and face uncovered. Draw the eyes.

4. Make boots out of black felt and glue them to the feet.

5. Glue on cotton for Santa's hair, beard, sleeves, and hat. For Santa's nose, make a little cotton ball and paint it.

6. Join the limbs to the body with the brads, using one set of small holes.

7. Run string through the remaining holes in the arms and legs, as shown.

8. Now gently pull the string and watch Santa dance!

💡 *Use your imagination:* *Make Mrs. Claus and some of Santa's helpers— and then put on a puppet play!*

19

A Jolly Santa Wreath

☛ YOU'LL NEED: *a paper plate, scissors, string, paint, a paintbrush, a pencil, pipe cleaners, glue, a marker, and tissue paper.*

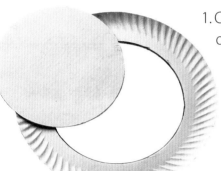

1. Cut out the bottom of a paper plate.

2. Paint the rim.

5. Wrap each circle around a pencil eraser. Dip each circle in glue and press it onto the rim, as shown.

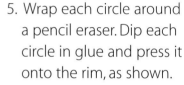

3. Draw a Santa Claus face on the cutout circle. Paint the face and cut it out.

4. Cut 1-inch circles out of tissue paper.

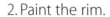

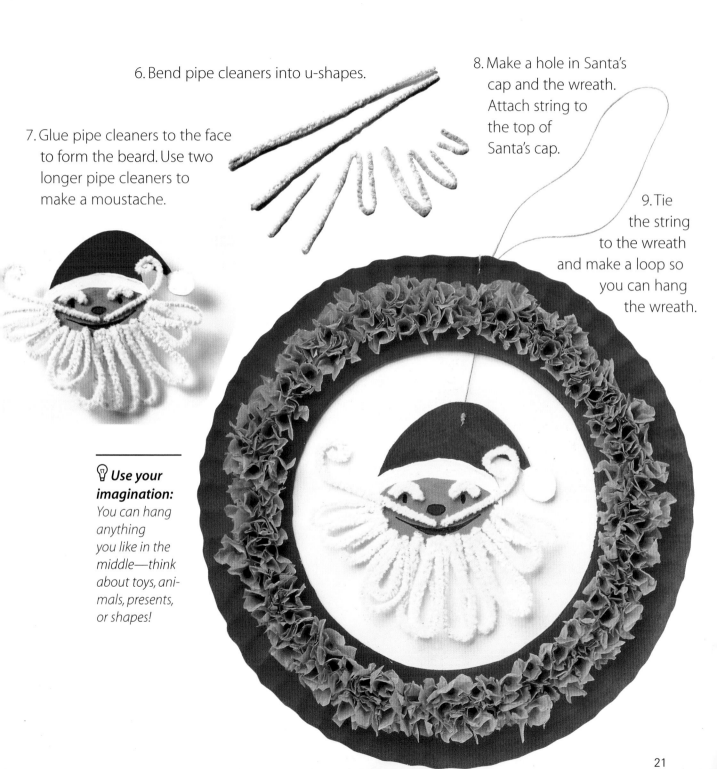

6. Bend pipe cleaners into u-shapes.

7. Glue pipe cleaners to the face to form the beard. Use two longer pipe cleaners to make a moustache.

8. Make a hole in Santa's cap and the wreath. Attach string to the top of Santa's cap.

9. Tie the string to the wreath and make a loop so you can hang the wreath.

💡 **Use your imagination:** You can hang anything you like in the middle—think about toys, animals, presents, or shapes!

21

Froggy Cardholder ✄

☛ *YOU'LL NEED: an egg carton, cardboard, marker, styrofoam, construction paper, cotton, glue, paints, utility knife, and scissors.*

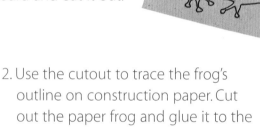

1. Draw the outline of a frog on cardboard and cut it out.

2. Use the cutout to trace the frog's outline on construction paper. Cut out the paper frog and glue it to the cardboard frog.

3. Cut out two compartments from an egg carton. Paint them white and draw a black circle in the center of each to make the frog's eyes.

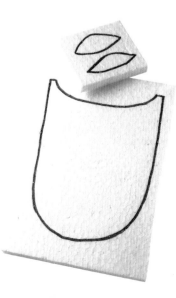

4. Find a piece of smooth styrofoam. Have an adult cut out the shape of a beard and a moustache with a utility knife.

5. Glue the egg containers to the face as eyes. Glue the beard and moustache to the body and face. Use a marker to draw the mouth and nostrils.

6. Make the cap out of a scrap of red cloth. Glue cotton to the cap for trim.

7. Put the cap on the frog and hang him in a visible place. If you like, attach Christmas cards to the beard.

💡 **Use your imagination:** *What other animals can you create? Add some more legs to make a spidery Santa or an octopus!*

Cute-as-a-Button Ornaments ✄

☛ *YOU'LL NEED: thin, corrugated cardboard, scraps of fabric, string, buttons, and wire or paper clips.*

1. Draw your favorite Christmas shapes on the smooth side of the cardboard.

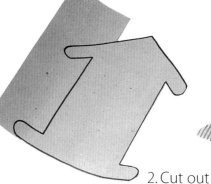

2. Cut out the shapes.

3. Cut out decorations, such as windows, doors, and tree trunks, from fabric scraps. Glue them to the cardboard cutouts.

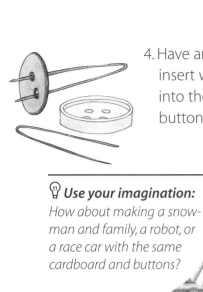

4. Have an adult help you insert wire or paper clips into the holes of different buttons.

💡 **Use your imagination:**
How about making a snow-man and family, a robot, or a race car with the same cardboard and buttons?

5. Stick the buttons through the cardboard and the cloth pieces. Glue a string hanger to the back of your ornament.

6. Now you're ready to decorate a tree, a window, or any other holiday space!

Ship of Good Cheer ✂

☞ *YOU'LL NEED: different-colored yarn, birthday candles, a small flashlight, cardboard, colored markers, glue, colored paper, tissue paper, shiny paper, thread, a stick, and scissors.*

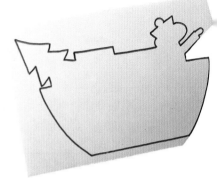

1. Draw the outline of a ship with its cargo on thick cardboard and cut it out.

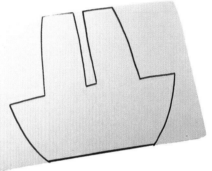

2. Trace the outline of a ship on another piece of cardboard, but add smokestacks.

3. Cut out the second outline with the smokestacks, and and color it with markers for the back of the ship.

4. Draw circles on the other cardboard outline and cut them out to make portholes. Paint the surface of the ship. Decorate the portholes. Fill the ship with gifts, a tree, and a sailor.

5. Glue tissue paper behind the portholes.

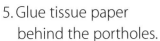

6. Glue the back of the ship to a 3-inch wide rectangular cardboard base and to two interior supports also glued to the base.

7. If you like, have an adult place three small candles, or a small flashlight, behind where the portholes will be.

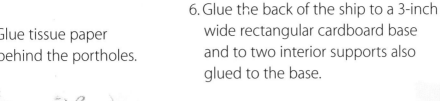

8. Make a star out of shiny silver paper. Run a thread through the tip of one of the star's points. Tie the thread to a stick for the sailor's fishing rod.

9. Glue the front of the ship to the base, and have an adult light the candles or shine the flashlight.

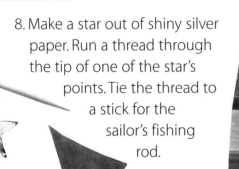

💡 **Use your imagination:**
How about making a car or a truck for your Christmas "trip" instead?

Heavenly Angels

☞ **YOU'LL NEED:**
colored cotton, paper clips, different-colored construction paper, black marker, glue, and scissors.

1. Draw the outline of an angel on construction paper, as shown.

2. Cut out the shape.

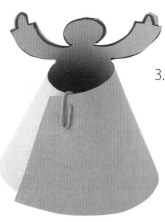

3. Fold the cutouts to form cones and fasten the ends with a paper clip at the top. Instead, you can make two vertical slits in the ends and insert one inside the other.

4. Glue cotton around the base of the angels.

28

5. Draw the eyes and mouth.

6. On a sheet of construction paper, draw the outline of wings. Cut them out and glue them onto the angels.

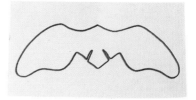

7. Cut out a paper rectangle and write the name of the person who will receive the angel. Glue it to the back of the angel's hands.

💡 **Use your imagination:** *Change the wing shapes and add headbands to make fairies, or add jewels and a crown to make snow queens.*

A Soaring Santa

☞ **YOU'LL NEED:**
*corrugated cardboard,
aluminum foil, a
marker, Christmas
stickers, glue, cord,
a wooden rod,
paper, cardboard,
and scissors.*

1. On two
pieces of cardboard,
draw a six-inch diameter
circle and a basket shape.

2. Cut out the two shapes
and cover the circle
with aluminum foil.

3. Cut corrugated cardboard
into one-inch-wide strips.
Then cut the
strips into
little squares.

4. Glue the squares on the basket
to make a checkerboard pattern
that covers the basket.

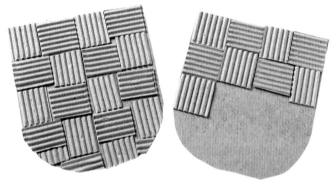

5. Cut out 24 little squares of aluminum foil. Place rolled-up paper in the middle of each square and tie with colored cord.

6. Draw a Santa Claus on cardboard, then color it and cut it out.

7. Use a rod or straw to join all the parts you've made. Decorate the balloon. Every day until the 25th of December, cut off one of the gifts hanging from the basket. Merry Christmas!

💡 **Use your imagination:**
Tuck messages or a tiny drawing inside each package for a special surprise each day!

WHERE TO GET SUPPLIES

Art & Woodcrafters Supply, Inc.
www.artwoodcrafter.com
Order a catalog or browse online for many different craft supplies.

Craft Supplies
www.craftsfaironline.com/Supplies.html
Features many different sites, each featuring products for specific hobbies.

Darice, Inc.
21160 Drake Road
Strongsville, OH 44136-6699
www.darice.com
Order a catalog or browse online for many different craft supplies.

Making Friends
www.makingfriends.com
Offers many kits and products for children's crafts.

National Artcraft
7996 Darrow Road
Twinsburg, OH 44087
www.nationalartcraft.com
This craft store features many products available through its catalog or online.

FOR MORE INFORMATION

Books

Chapman, Gillian. Pam Robson (Contributor). *Art From Fabric: With Projects Using Rags, Old Clothes, and Remnants.* New York, NY: Thomson Learning, 1995.

Chapman, Gillian. *Autumn* (Seasonal Crafts). Chatham, NJ: Raintree/Steck Vaughn, 1997.

Connor, Nikki. Sarah Jean Neaves (Illustrator). *Cardboard Boxes* (Creating Crafts From). Providence, RI: Copper Beech Books, 1996.

Gordon, Lynn. *52 Great Art Projects For Kids.* San Francisco, CA: Chronicle Books, 1996.

King, Penny. Clare Roundhill (Contributor). *Animals* (Artists' Workshop). New York, NY: Crabtree Publishing, 1996.

Ross, Kathy. Sharon Lane Holm (Illustrator). *The Best Holiday Crafts Ever.* Brookfield, CT: Millbrook Publishing, 1996.

Smith, Alistair. *Big Book of Papercraft.* Newton, MA: Educational Development Center, 1996.

Video

Blue's Clues Arts & Crafts. Nickelodeon. (1998).

Web Sites

Crafts For Kids
www.craftsforkids.miningco.com/mbody.htm
Many different arts and crafts activities are explained in detail.

Family Crafts
www.family.go.com
Search for crafts by age group. Projects include instructions, supply list, and helpful tips.

KinderCrafts
www.EnchantedLearning.com/Crafts
Step-by-step instructions explain how to make animal, dinosaur, box, and paper crafts, plus much more.

Making Friends
www.makingfriends.com
Contains hundreds of craft ideas with detailed instructions for children ages 2 to 12, including paper dolls, summer crafts, yucky stuff, and holiday crafts.

INDEX